ALTERNATOR
BOOKS™

TECH·TITANS

THE GENIUS OF
APPLE

How Tim Cook and Personal Computing Changed the World

Margaret J. Goldstein

Lerner Publications ◆ Minneapolis

Lerner Publications Company
An imprint of Lerner Publishing Group, Inc.
241 First Avenue North
Minneapolis, MN 55401 USA

For reading levels and more information, look up this title at www.lernerbooks.com.

Main body text set in Aptifer Sans LT Pro.
Typeface provided by Linotype AG.

Library of Congress Cataloging-in-Publication Data

Names: Goldstein, Margaret J., author.
Title: The genius of Apple : how Tim Cook and personal computing changed the
    world / Margaret J. Goldstein.
Description: Minneapolis : Lerner Publications, [2022] | Series: Tech titans
    (Alternator books) | Includes bibliographical references and index. | Audience:
    Ages 8–12 | Audience: Grades 4–6 | Summary: "Since Steve Jobs helped found
    Apple in 1976, the company has been at the cutting edge of computing,
    introducing the world to personal computers, the iPhone, and more. Learn about
    Apple's past, present, and future"— Provided by publisher.
Identifiers: LCCN 2021020584 (print) | LCCN 2021020585 (ebook) |
    ISBN 9781728440828 (library binding) | ISBN 9781728449517 (paperback) |
    ISBN 9781728445243 (ebook)
Subjects: LCSH: Apple Computer, Inc.—Juvenile literature. | Cook, Timothy D.,
    1960—-Juvenile literature. | Computer industry—United States—History—
    Juvenile literature.
Classification: LCC HD9696.2.U64 A67334 2022 (print) | LCC HD9696.2.U64 (ebook) |
    DDC 338.7/610040973—dc23

LC record available at https://lccn.loc.gov/2021020584
LC ebook record available at https://lccn.loc.gov/2021020585

Manufactured in the United States of America
1 – CG – 7/15/22

TABLE OF CONTENTS

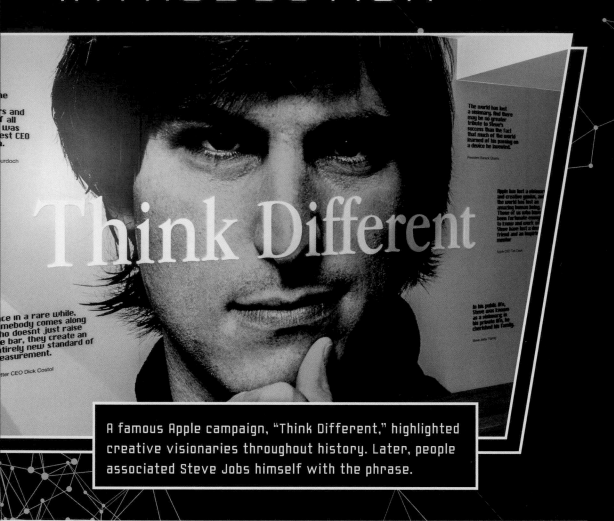

A famous Apple campaign, "Think Different," highlighted creative visionaries throughout history. Later, people associated Steve Jobs himself with the phrase.

In 1979, the personal computing industry was just getting started. The first personal computers had come on the market only a few years earlier. Using these computers could be frustrating. To operate them, users had to type in symbols and codes. Monitors displayed only letters, numbers, and other characters.

Steve Jobs, cofounder and head of Apple Computer Company, wanted to make personal computing easier and more exciting. In December 1979, he and other Apple staffers met with engineers at the Palo Alto Research Center (PARC), not far from Apple's offices in California. At PARC, Jobs saw a new approach to computing. Engineers had designed a computer with a graphical user interface (GUI). Instead of typing characters and codes to run the machine, users clicked on icons with a mouse. Instead of displaying only numbers, letters, and symbols, the computer displayed multicolor pictures.

Immediately, Jobs knew he had seen the future of personal computing. He declared that Apple would build a GUI into its new machines. That decision revolutionized the personal computer industry.

PARC is owned by Xerox.

In the 1960s, computers were made up of several pieces of heavy equipment.

CHAPTER 1:
THE BEGINNING

Growing up in San Jose, California, Steve Wozniak loved science. His dad was an aerospace engineer. He taught Steve about electronics and radios. In the 1960s, at Homestead High School in Cupertino, California, Wozniak became interested in computers. At that time, computers were large,

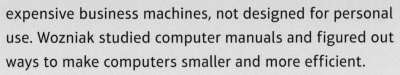

expensive business machines, not designed for personal use. Wozniak studied computer manuals and figured out ways to make computers smaller and more efficient.

   After high school, Wozniak attended college in Colorado and California. In 1971 he met Jobs, who was still in high school at Homestead. The two shared a love of electronics. They used their technical skills to build illegal devices called blue boxes. These allowed users to hack into the phone system to make free long-distance calls. Wozniak and Jobs sold dozens of their blue boxes and were never caught.

Steve Wozniak in 1968

APPLE I

Wozniak took a job designing calculators at Hewlett Packard. Jobs, after attending Reed College in Oregon for a time, worked at Atari, a video game company.

In 1975, Wozniak joined the Homebrew Computer Club. Members swapped tips on building their own personal computers. Some Homebrew members bought an Altair 8800. They had to assemble the computer themselves. It didn't have a keyboard or a monitor. To load software, input data, and display results, users

A 1975 Altair 8800 computer

An original Apple I computer in a briefcase

had to link the computer with expensive external devices. Wozniak had a better idea. He designed a computer that worked nearly right out of the box. It had a keyboard for inputting data and hooked up to an ordinary TV as a monitor.

Wozniak freely shared his computer design with the Homebrew Club. But Jobs said they should sell Wozniak's computer instead. Wozniak agreed, and they formed the Apple Computer Company. The name was inspired by Jobs' time working at an apple orchard. They called their first computer the Apple I.

BIG BUSINESS

By modern standards, the Apple I was primitive.
Its casing was made of wood. It could not display
different colors or play sound, and it had no drive for
storing data. Apple produced only a few hundred of
these computers.

The company's next machine, Apple II, was released
in 1977. It had a hard plastic casing, a color monitor,
and a floppy disk drive. It had more memory than the
Apple I, ports for attaching printers and other devices,

Jobs, Apple CEO John Sculley, and Wozniak
(*left to right*) unveiled the Apple IIc computer
in April 1984. The "c" stood for "compact."

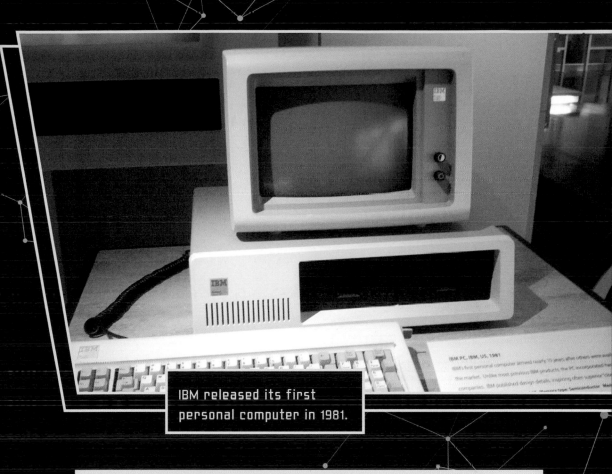

IBM released its first
personal computer in 1981.

and a sound system. With an Apple II, a user could edit
text, keep track of personal or business finances, and
play games. Instead of only computer hobbyists, Apple II
customers came from all walks of life.

In the early 1980s, the home computer market exploded.
Customers rushed to buy computers from Apple and other
companies.

One of Apple's biggest competitors was IBM, a large
business machine company. IBM sold more computers
than Apple, but Apple was a leader in other ways.

Apple engineers kept improving their GUI. They built the Lisa, a computer with a GUI-based operating system (OS). Released in 1983, the Lisa was expensive and didn't sell well. The following year, Apple introduced its smaller, lower-priced Macintosh, which also featured a GUI. Users loved it. They could drag and drop files and folders, click on icons and menus, and create colorful graphics and type. The Macintosh was a winner, and sales were strong.

The Macintosh computer came with a 9-inch (23 cm) screen, keyboard, and single-button mouse.

APPLE VS. MICROSOFT

Apple and Microsoft have long been rivals. The rivalry started when IBM released its first personal computer in 1981. It had an OS built by Microsoft. Most other computer makers also chose Microsoft's OS, so Microsoft became the standard for personal computing. Apple used its own OS.

Microsoft-based machines were less expensive than Apple computers, and that appealed to many buyers. To compete with the Macintosh's popular GUI OS, Microsoft built its own GUI OS, Windows. In 1995, Microsoft released the extremely popular Windows 95. This further cemented the company's lead over Apple.

In the 2020s, Microsoft still dominates personal computing. Its market share for desktop computers is 80 percent, compared to just 7.5 percent for Apple. In revenue, however, Apple is on top. In 2020, Apple took in $275 billion, compared to about $143 billion for Microsoft.

Windows on a Microsoft Surface tablet

Their company had made them famous and wealthy, but by 1985, Wozniak and Jobs were ready for a change. Both left Apple that year. Wozniak started CL 9, a company that built remote controls for TVs. Jobs launched NeXT, which built computer hardware and software. He also headed Pixar Animation Studios for a time. Jobs didn't stay away from Apple forever, though. In 1996, Apple bought NeXT. The following year, Jobs returned as Apple's chief executive officer (CEO).

THE STEVE JOBS BUILDING

Pixar renamed its main building the Steve Jobs Building in 2012.

Jobs introduced the NeXTcube workstation in 1990. The computer was a perfect cube, which made it difficult to manufacture.

Newer iPad models can mirror or extend the desktop of a Mac.

CHAPTER 2:
STANDOUT PRODUCTS

A lot has changed since Jobs and Wozniak founded Apple Computer Company. In 2007, the company name was shortened to Apple. By 2021, Apple was worth more than $2 trillion.

Apple sells Mac desktop computers, MacBook laptops, and iPad tablets. It also sells iPod portable music players.

Most Apple computers come preloaded with software, such as Pages for word processing, Numbers for making spreadsheets, and Garage Band for recording music. Popular Microsoft programs also work on Macs. Safari is Apple's web browser. Its music streaming service is Apple Music, and its video streaming service is Apple TV.

MONEY IN THE BANK

Introduced in 2007, the iPhone, a smartphone, is Apple's most popular product. It was the first mobile phone with a full internet connection. Around the world, more than one billion people own iPhones. Booming iPhone sales have made Apple one of the richest companies in the world.

To buy an Apple product, customers can order online or visit an Apple Store. They can take broken devices to the Genius Bar inside Apple Stores for repairs.

The first-generation iPhone from 2007 (*right*) and the iPhone 12 Pro, which came out in 2020

APPLE WATCH

The Apple Watch is like a wearable iPhone. It has apps for texting, playing music, surfing the web, and more. But its main use is as a health and fitness monitor. The device can measure the wearer's heart rate and oxygen levels. It can track how many miles the wearer walks and how many calories are burned during a workout. If the watch senses that the wearer has fallen or been hurt, it can even contact emergency services.

The Activity app on the Apple Watch shows three rings. They represent calories burned, minutes of brisk activity, and amount of time spent standing and moving around. The goal is to close all three rings each day.

Apple retail stores are known for their clean and simple displays that let the products shine. Worldwide, Apple Stores reportedly welcome more than one million visitors a day!

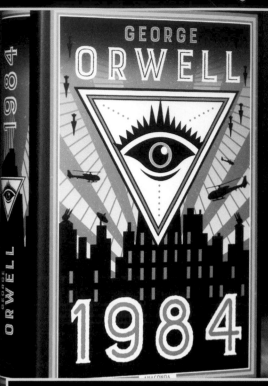

George Orwell's *1984* came out in 1949. It is a cautionary tale about government surveillance and oppression.

CHAPTER 3:
IN THE NEWS

Apple has long been a newsmaker. In 1984, it produced a dramatic TV ad to introduce the Macintosh. The ad, which ran during the Super Bowl, featured an athlete with a sledgehammer being pursued by police. She smashed a giant TV screen showing Big Brother, the symbol of an all-powerful government from George Orwell's classic novel *1984*. The ad represented a small but fearless Apple computer striking a blow for freedom and creativity.

Jobs also made headlines. He was an aggressive business leader who often clashed with other Apple executives. In 2004, Jobs announced that he had pancreatic cancer. He continued running Apple even as he grew sicker. He died in 2011. Tim Cook, Apple's chief operating officer, took over as CEO after Jobs died.

People left flowers and apples outside Apple Stores to honor Jobs after his death.

MAKING AN IMPACT

When Apple introduces new products, it rolls out big media campaigns to create buzz. The world first learned about the iPhone at Macworld 2007. There, Jobs announced that Apple was combining an iPod, a cell phone, and internet-connection into one device. Apple followed up with heavy advertising for the iPhone. When the first iPhones went on sale seven months later, customers stood in line for hours to buy one.

Jobs introduced the MacBook Air at the 2008 Macworld event.

Customers in New York City waited in line for blocks to purchase the iPhone 6 in 2014.

Apple users love their devices, but the company has critics too. In 2017, lawyers charged that Apple was deliberately misleading people who owned iPhone 6 and 7 models. Their phones were running slowly and shutting off unexpectedly. When that happened, many people spent hundreds of dollars on new iPhones. What Apple didn't reveal was that users just needed a new twenty-nine-dollar battery in their old phones. In a series of lawsuits, judges ruled against Apple. In the settlement, Apple agreed to pay millions of dollars in compensation, although individual consumers would only receive an estimated twenty-five dollars each.

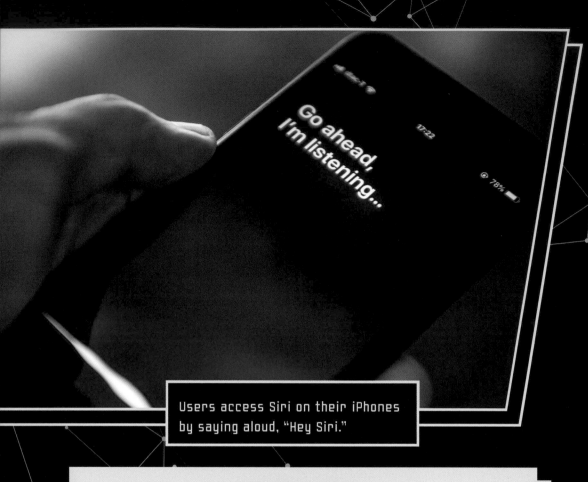

Users access Siri on their iPhones by saying aloud, "Hey Siri."

CHAPTER 4:
A LOOK AHEAD

Artificial intelligence (AI) is part of many Apple products. For instance, Apple devices can turn handwriting into typed text and typed text into spoken words. They can also translate one language into another. Siri, Apple's digital assistant, responds to voice commands. You can tell Siri to dial a phone number, send a text, give a traffic report, set a timer, play your favorite music, turn on the lights, search the web, and much more.

More AI will be part of Apple's future. But AI poses privacy concerns. Siri is helpful, but it collects a lot of data. It can record users' conversations, track their locations, and monitor their likes and dislikes. Consumer groups have pushed back, demanding that Apple build more privacy protection into Siri and other software.

Apple's HomePod mini is a smart speaker that plays music and offers voice assistance from Siri.

Apple is also at the forefront of augmented reality (AR). With AR-enabled devices, users can see "inside" objects and living things, design spaces, play games, and much more. Apple hopes to release a virtual reality (VR) headset in 2022. It will immerse users in 3D digital environments for gaming, video-watching, job training, and other activities.

Apple hopes to one day produce an electric car, perhaps one that can drive itself. Apple engineers are developing batteries, new AI technology, sensors, and other systems to make the car a reality.

PlayStation is an established competitor in the AR market. It released its first VR headset in 2016.

FACE AND TOUCH ID

Computer users generally use passwords to access devices and apps. But Apple offers alternatives. Apple's Face ID lets you unlock an Apple device just by looking at it. The system compares your face to a previously loaded picture. If the two match, you get access. Apple's Touch ID is similar. You touch a sensor on your device. The system compares your fingerprint to a fingerprint on file. The device opens if the fingerprints match.

How to Set Up Face ID
First, position your face in the camera frame. Then move your head in a circle to show all the angles of your face.

Get Started

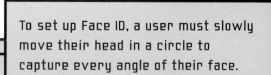

To set up Face ID, a user must slowly move their head in a circle to capture every angle of their face.

TIMELINE

1976: Steve Jobs and Steve Wozniak found the Apple Computer Company.

1977: Apple releases the Apple II, its first widely sold computer.

1983: Apple releases the Lisa, its first computer with GUI.

1984: Apple introduces the Macintosh with a big media campaign.

1985: Jobs and Wozniak leave Apple.

1997: Jobs returns to Apple.

2007: Apple introduces the iPhone.

2011: Jobs dies of pancreatic cancer.

2014: Apple introduces the Apple Watch.

2021: Apple is valued at more than $2 trillion.

GLOSSARY

artificial intelligence (AI): a computer system that imitates human thought to process information

augmented reality (AR): an experience that combines real-world sights, sounds, and activities with computer-generated information

digital assistant: software that performs tasks, such as sending text messages, searching the web, or controlling electronic devices, in response to voice commands

graphical user interface (GUI): software that allows users to control their computers by clicking on icons or menu items rather than typing in commands

market share: the percentage of total sales of a certain type of product generated by a particular company

operating system (OS): software that controls programs, memory, and the flow of information into and out of a computer

personal computer: a small computer designed to be operated by one person

revenue: income earned by a business

virtual reality (VR): an artificial environment with sounds and sights created by a computer

LEARN MORE

Apple
https://www.apple.com/

Gitlin, Martin. *Wearable Electronics*. Ann Arbor, MI: Cherry Lake, 2018.

Goldstein, Margaret J. *The Genius of Microsoft: How Bill Gates and Windows Changed the World*. Minneapolis: Lerner Publications, 2022.

Hayes, Amy. *Tim Cook: Industrial Engineer and CEO of Apple*. New York: PowerKids, 2018.

Klepeis, Alicia Z. *How Smartphones Work*. New York: Cavendish Square, 2019.

Steve Jobs
https://easyscienceforkids.com/facts-about-steve-jobs/

Steve Wozniak Facts for Kids
https://kids.kiddle.co/Steve_Wozniak

Tim Cook Facts for Kids
https://kids.kiddle.co/Tim_Cook

INDEX

PHOTO ACKNOWLEDGMENTS

The images in this book are used with the permission of: © Anton_Ivanov/Shutterstock Images, p. 4; © Tada Images/Shutterstock Images, p. 5; © UC Davis College of Engineering/Flickr, p. 6; © Homestead High School/Wikimedia Commons, p. 7; © Tim Colegrove/Wikimedia Commons, p. 8; © Binarysequence/Wikimedia Commons, p. 9; © Sal Veder/AP Images, p. 10; © Travis Wise/Flickr, p. 11; © audioundwerbung/iStockphoto, p. 12; © Kārlis Dambrāns/Wikimedia Commons, p. 13; © Ben Terrett/Flickr, p. 14; © Simon Claessen/Flickr, p. 15; © Chaay_Tee/iStockphoto, p. 16; © marleyPug/Shutterstock Images, p. 17 (first-generation iPhone); © neirfy/iStockphoto, p. 17 (iPhone 12 pro); © Alexey Boldin/Shutterstock Images, p. 18; © emasali stock/Shutterstock Images, p. 19; © Palatinate Stock/Shutterstock Images, p. 20; © josanmu/iStockphoto, p. 21; © Aljawad/Wikimedia Commons, p. 22; © robertcicchetti/iStockphoto, p. 23; © Wachiwit/Shutterstock Images, p. 24; © Ugis Riba/Shutterstock Images, p. 25; © EQRoy/Shutterstock Images, p. 26; © DenPhotos/Shutterstock Images, p. 27.

Cover Photos: © Erik Pendzich/Alamy Photo (Tim Cook); © neirfy/iStockphoto (iPhone 12 pro); © Nikada/iStockphoto (Apple Store)

Design Elements: © Hluboki Dzianis/Shutterstock Images